MMO CD
3820
MMO Cass.
8131

S LAUREATE

MUSIC MINUS ONE
INTERMEDIATE
CONTEST SOLOS

SERIES

TRUMPET
MUSIC BOOK

A Tune for Christopher

Art Dedrick

Thème Varié

Robert Clérisse

Per La Gloria D'Adorarri from 'Griselda'

Giovanni Bononcini

Concertino

Adagio

G. F. Handel
Arr. A. W. Benoy

COMPACT DISC PAGE AND BAND INFORMATION

MMO CD 3820
MMO Cass. 8131

 Music Minus One

LAUREATE SERIES CONTEST SOLOS
BEGINNING LEVEL FOR TRUMPET, VOL. 3

PERFORMANCE GUIDE

ART DEDRICK
A Tune for Christopher

To me, this composition seems to fall into the category of a lullaby. It should be played as one would sing a song, with the notes very well connected. Using the syllable "du" for articulation will help maintain that character. Note the little excitement that appears at letter B, and then return to the original feeling at letter C.

ROBERT CLÉRISSE
Thème Varié

As the composer indicates, the first section should be played with much energy and pomp. Articulations must be very precise and definite for best effect.

The *Andantino* is somewhat stylized, as the composer suggests when he writes, "in the style of a popular song." The articulation here is softer than that in the first section, and there is more freedom in the beat. The cadenza at the end of this part is executed in a fashion that seems to continue the mood of the music directly preceding it.

The third section is a return to the style of the first— energetic and well articulated. This piece should be a pleasure to play. It has much variety and provides a good vehicle for expressing one's own personality.

GIOVANNI BONONCINI
Per La Gloria D'Adorarri from "Griselda"

This is a lovely setting of a beautiful song, which should make you feel like you are singing as you play your trumpet. Dynamic markings are important; full use of the *crescendi* and *decrescendi* will make your playing especially effective. Place the grace notes in measures 39 and 43 on the beat, a tradition with music of this period.

G. F. HANDEL
Concertino

This work is divided into four sections. The first part, *Adagio*, should be played in a stately fashion, with all notes placed exactly where they belong. Dynamic markings are important to the continuing interest of the piece.

Minuet, the second section, should be thought of as a slow waltz, a dance form in 3/4 time. The flow from loud to soft will keep the music moving and lend animation to your playing.

The *Sarabande* starts out with a strong trumpet statement that sets the mood for the austerity and dignity of the piece. Again, well placed notes in perfect time are of the utmost importance.

The *Finale* is the most technical of all the movements of the *Concertino*. It should be played as a march, almost pompous in character. Listen carefully to the phrasing and articulation in the four measures before letter A. At letter B, the second quarter note in each of the first two measures is held a bit longer than normal to minimize the length of the silence on the third and fourth beats.

Raymond Crisara

TUNING

Before the piano accompaniment begins you will hear four tuning notes, followed by a short scale and another tuning note. This will enable you to tune your instrument to the record.

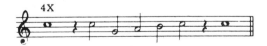

A Tune for Christopher

Cassette

SIDE B - BAND 1

Compact Disc
Band 1 - With Trumpet
Band 9 - Without Trumpet

Art Dedrick

MMO CD 3820
MMO Cass. 8131

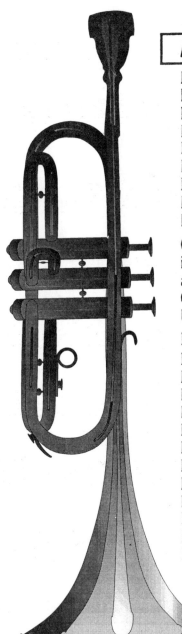

Music Minus One TRUMPET Compact Discs

MMO CD 3801 3 Trumpet Concerti   Handel/Telemann/Vivaldi
MMO CD 3802 Easy Solos, Student Edition, **Beginning** Level vol. 1
MMO CD 3803 Easy Solos, Student Edition, **Beginning** Level vol. 2
MMO CD 3804 Easy Jazz Duets with Rhythm **Section,** Beginning Level
MMO CD 3805 Music for Brass Ensemble
MMO CD 3806 First Chair Trumpet Solos
MMO CD 3807 The Art Of The Solo Trumpet
MMO CD 3808 Baroque Brass And Beyond
MMO CD 3809 The Arban Duets

Choice selections for the Trumpet, drawn from the **very best** solo literature for the instrument. The pieces are performed by the foremost virtuosi of our time, artists affiliated with the New York Philharmonic, Boston, Chicago, Cleveland and Philadelphia Orchestras, The Juilliard School, Curtis Institute of Music, Indiana University, University of Toronto and Metropolitan Opera Orchestra.

Beginning	Intermediate Advanced	Level
MMO CD 3811	Gerard Schwarz, N.Y. Philharmonic	B
MMO CD 3812	Armando Ghitalla, Boston Symphony	B
MMO CD 3813	Robert Nagel, Soloist, **NY Brass** Ensemble	I
MMO CD 3814	Gerard Schwarz, N.Y. Philharmonic	I
MMO CD 3815	Robert Nagel, Soloist NY Brass Ensemble	A
MMO CD 3816	Armando Ghitalla, Boston Symphony	I
MMO CD 3817	Gerard Schwarz, N.Y. Philharmonic	I
MMO CD 3818	Robert Nagel, Soloist, **NY Brass** Ensemble	A
MMO CD 3819	Armando Ghitalla, Boston Symphony	A
MMO CD 3820	Raymond Crisara, Concert Soloist	B
MMO CD 3821	Raymond Crisara, Concert Soloist	B
MMO CD 3822	Raymond Crisara, Concert Soloist	I

Cassette
SIDE B - BAND 2

Compact Disc
Band 2 - With Trumpet
Band 10 - Without Trumpet

Thème Varié

Robert Clérisse

4 taps (2 measures) precede music.

MMO CD 3820
MMO Cass. 8131

Per La Gloria D'Adorarri from 'Griselda'

Cassette

SIDE B - BAND 3

Giovanni Bononcini

Compact Disc
Band 3 - With Trumpet
Band 11 - Without Trumpet

MMO CD 3820
MMO Cass. 8131

Concertino

Adagio

Cassette

Total time: 10'40"

Compact Disc
Band 4 - With Trumpet
Band 12 - Without Trumpet

G. F. Handel
Arr. A. W. Benoy

SIDE B - BAND 4   ♩ = 69 (3'50")

MMO CD 3820
MMO Cass. 8131

Finale

Cassette

SIDE B - BAND 7

Compact Disc
Band 7 - With Trumpet
Band 15 - Without Trumpet

MUSIC MINUS ONE COMPACT DISC CATALOG

Music Minus One PIANO Compact Discs

__ MMO CD 3001 Beethoven Piano Concerto No. 1 in C, Opus 15
__ MMO CD 3002 Beethoven Piano Concerto No. 2 in Bb, Opus 19
__ MMO CD 3003 Beethoven Piano Concerto No. 3 in Cm, Opus 37
__ MMO CD 3004 Beethoven Piano Concerto No. 4 in G, Opus 58
__ MMO CD 3005 Beethoven Piano Concerto No. 5 in Eb, Opus 73
__ MMO CD 3006 Grieg Piano Concerto in A minor, Opus 16
__ MMO CD 3007 Rachmaninoff Piano Concerto No. 2 in C minor
__ MMO CD 3008 Schumann Piano Concerto in A minor, Opus 54
__ MMO CD 3009 Brahms Piano Concerto No. 1 in D minor, Opus 15
__ MMO CD 3010 Chopin Piano Concerto No. 1 in Em, Opus 11
__ MMO CD 3011 Mendelssohn Piano Concerto No. 1 in Gm, Opus 25
__ MMO CD 3012 W.A. Mozart Piano Concerto No. 9 in Ebm, K.271
__ MMO CD 3013 W.A. Mozart Piano Concerto No. 12 in A, K.414
__ MMO CD 3014 W.A. Mozart Piano Concerto No. 20 in Dm, K.466
__ MMO CD 3015 W.A. Mozart Piano Concerto No. 23 in A, K.488
__ MMO CD 3016 W.A. Mozart Piano Concerto No. 24 in Cm, K.491
__ MMO CD 3017 W.A. Mozart Piano Concerto No. 26 in D, 'Coronation'
__ MMO CD 3018 W.A. Mozart Piano Concerto in G major, K.453
__ MMO CD 3019 Liszt Piano Concerto No. 1/Weber Concertstucke
__ MMO CD 3020 Liszt Piano Concerto No. 2/Hungarian Fantasia
__ MMO CD 3021 J.S. Bach Piano Concerto in Fm/J.C. Bach Concerto in Eb
__ MMO CD 3022 J.S. Bach Piano Concerto in D minor
__ MMO CD 3023 Haydn Piano Concerto in D major
__ MMO CD 3024 Heart Of The Piano Concerto
__ MMO CD 3025 Themes From The Great Piano Concerti
__ MMO CD 3026 Tschiakowsky Piano Concerto No. 1 in Bbm, Opus 23
__ MMO CD 3027 Rachmaninoff: Six Scenes for 4 Hands
__ MMO CD 3028 Arensky: Six Pieces
              Stravinsky: 3 Dances: March/Valse/Polka
__ MMO CD 3029 Faure: Dolly Suite - 4 hands
__ MMO CD 3031 Schumann: Pictures from the East
              6 Impromptus for 4 hands
__ MMO CD 3032 Beethoven: Three Marches, Op. 45 4 hands

Music Minus One VOCALIST Compact Discs

__ MMO CD 4001 Schubert Lieder for High Voice
__ MMO CD 4002 Schubert Lieder for Low Voice
__ MMO CD 4003 Schubert Lieder for High Voice   volume 2
__ MMO CD 4004 Schubert Lieder for Low Voice   volume 2
__ MMO CD 4005 Brahms Lieder for High Voice
__ MMO CD 4006 Brahms Lieder for Low Voice
__ MMO CD 4007 Everybody's Favorite Songs for High Voice
__ MMO CD 4008 Everybody's Favorite Songs for Low Voice
__ MMO CD 4009 Everybody's Favorite Songs for High Voice   volume 2
__ MMO CD 4010 Everybody's Favorite Songs for Low Voice   volume 2
__ MMO CD 4011 17th/18th Century Italian Songs High Voice
__ MMO CD 4012 17th/18th Century Italian Songs Low Voice
__ MMO CD 4013 17th/18th Century Italian Songs High Voice   volume 2
__ MMO CD 4014 17th/18th Century Italian Songs Low Voice   volume 2
__ MMO CD 4015 Famous Soprano Arias
__ MMO CD 4016 Famous Mezzo-Soprano Arias
__ MMO CD 4017 Famous Tenor Arias
__ MMO CD 4018 Famous Baritone Arias
__ MMO CD 4019 Famous Bass Arias
__ MMO CD 4020 Hugo Wolf Lieder for High Voice
__ MMO CD 4021 Hugo Wolf Lieder for Low Voice
__ MMO CD 4022 Richard Strauss Lieder for High Voice
__ MMO CD 4023 Richard Strauss Lieder for Low Voice
__ MMO CD 4024 Robert Schumann Lieder for High Voice
__ MMO CD 4025 Robert Schumann Lieder for Low Voice
__ MMO CD 4026 W.A. Mozart Arias For Soprano
__ MMO CD 4027 Verdi Arias For Soprano
__ MMO CD 4028 Italian Arias For Soprano
__ MMO CD 4029 French Arias For Soprano
__ MMO CD 4030 Soprano Oratorio Arias
__ MMO CD 4031 Alto Oratorio Arias
__ MMO CD 4032 Tenor Oratorio Arias
__ MMO CD 4033 Bass Oratorio Arias

Choice selections for the Vocalist, drawn from the very best solo literature for the voice. Professional artists perform these pieces to guide the singer in interpreting each piece.

*MMO CD 4041 Beginning Soprano Solos   Kate Hurney, soprano
*MMO CD 4042 Intermediate Soprano Solos   Kate Hurney, soprano
*MMO CD 4043 Beginning Mezzo Sop. Solos   Fay Kittelson, mezzo-sop.
*MMO CD 4044 Intermediate Mezzo-Sop. Solos   Fay Kittelson, mezzo-sop.
*MMO CD 4045 Advanced Mezzo-Sop. Solos   Fay, Kittelson, mezzo-sop.
*MMO CD 4046 Beginning Contralto Solos   Carline Ray, mezzo-sop.
*MMO CD 4047 Beginning Tenor Solos   George Shirley, tenor
*MMO CD 4048 Intermediate Tenor Solos   George Shirley, tenor
*MMO CD 4049 Advance Tenor Solos   George Shirley, tenor

*Winter/'95   Spring/'96 Release

Music Minus One CELLO Compact Discs

__ MMO CD 3701 Dvorak: Cello Concerto in B minor, Opus 104
__ MMO CD 3702 C.P.E. Bach: Cello Concerto in A minor
__ MMO CD 3703 Boccherini: Concerto in Bb Major; Bruch: Kol Nidrei

Music Minus One GUITAR Compact Discs

__ MMO CD 3601 Boccherini: Guitar Quintet, No. 4 in D major
__ MMO CD 3602 Giuliani: Guitar Quintet, Opus 65
__ MMO CD 3603 Classic Guitar Duets Easy - Medium
__ MMO CD 3604 Renaissance & Baroque Guitar Duets
__ MMO CD 3605 Classical & Romantic Guitar Duets
__ MMO CD 3606 Guitar & Flute Duets, vol. 1
__ MMO CD 3607 Guitar & Flute Duets, vol. 2
__ MMO CD 3608 Bluegrass Guitar

Music Minus One FLUTE Compact Discs

__ MMO CD 3300 Mozart Concerto in D/Quantz Concerto in G
__ MMO CD 3301 Mozart Flute Concerto in G major
__ MMO CD 3302 J.S. Bach Suite No. 2 in Bm

The repertoire and editions used in the Laureate Series correspond to the approved music lists of various Music Education Associations and may be performed as contest solos in State Music Festivals. Contest regulations, such as time limitations have been taken into consideration.

__ MMO CD 3303 Boccherini/Vivaldi Concerti/Mozart Andante
__ MMO CD 3304 Haydn/Vivaldi/Frederick "The Great" Concerti
__ MMO CD 3305 Vivaldi/Telemann/Leclair Flute Concerti
__ MMO CD 3306 J.S. Bach Brandenburg No. 2/Haydn Concerto
__ MMO CD 3307 J.S. Bach Triple Concerto/Vivaldi Concerto No. 9
__ MMO CD 3308 Mozart/Stamitz Flute Quartets
__ MMO CD 3309 Haydn London Trios
__ MMO CD 3310 J.S. Bach Brandenburg Concerti No. 4 and No. 5
__ MMO CD 3311 W.A. Mozart Three Flute Quartets
__ MMO CD 3312 Telemann Am Suite/Gluck 'Orpheus' Scene/Pergolesi Conc. in G
__ MMO CD 3313 Flute Song Easy familiar Classics
__ MMO CD 3314 Vivaldi 3 Flute Concerti RV 427, 438, Opus 10 No. 5
__ MMO CD 3315 Vivaldi 3 Flute Concerti RV 440, Opus 10 No. 4, RV 429
__ MMO CD 3316 Easy Solos, Student Editions, Beginning Level vol. 1
__ MMO CD 3317 Easy Solos, Student Editions, Beginning Level vol. 2
__ MMO CD 3318 Easy Jazz Duets, Student Editions, 1-3 years
__ MMO CD 3319 Flute & Guitar Duets, vol. 1
__ MMO CD 3320 Flute & Guitar Duets, vol. 2
__ MMO CD 3333 First Chair Flute Solos With Orchestra

Choice selections for the Flute, drawn from the very best solo literature for the instrument. The pieces are performed by the foremost virtuosi of our time, artists affiliated with the New York Philharmonic, Boston, Chicago, Cleveland and Philadelphia Orchestras, The Juilliard School, Curtis Institute of Music, Indiana University, University of Toronto and Metropolitan Opera Orchestra.

	Beginning	Intermediate	Advanced	Level
__ MMO CD 3321		Murray Pantiz, Philadelphia Orch.		B
__ MMO CD 3322		Donald Peck, Chicago Symphony		B
__ MMO CD 3323		Julius Baker, N.Y. Philharmonic		I
__ MMO CD 3324		Donald Peck, Chicago Symphony		I
__ MMO CD 3325		Murray Panitz, Philadelphia Orch.		A
__ MMO CD 3326		Julius Baker, N.Y. Philharmonic		A
__ MMO CD 3327		Donald Peck, Chicago Symphony		I
__ MMO CD 3328		Murray Panitz, Philadelphia Orch.		A
__ MMO CD 3329		Julius Baker, N.Y. Philharmonic		I
__ MMO CD 3330		Doriot Dwyer, Boston Symphony		B
__ MMO CD 3331		Doriot Dwyer, Boston Symphony		I
__ MMO CD 3332		Doriot Dwyer, Boston Symphony		A

Music Minus One FRENCH HORN Compact Discs

__ MMO CD 3501 Mozart: Concerto No. 2, K.417; No. 3, K.447

Choice selections for the French Horn, drawn from the very best solo literature for the instrument. The pieces are performed by the foremost virtuosi of our time, artists affiliated with the New York Philharmonic, Boston, Chicago, Cleveland and Philadelphia Orchestras, The Juilliard School, Curtis Institute of Music, Indiana University, University of Toronto and Metropolitan Opera Orchestra.

	Beginning	Intermediate	Advanced	Level
__ MMO CD 3502		Baroque Brass And Beyond		
__ MMO CD 3503		Music For Brass Ensemble		
__ MMO CD 3511		Mason Jones, Philadelphia Orch.		B
__ MMO CD 3512		Myron Bloom, Cleveland Symphony		B
__ MMO CD 3513		Dale Clevenger, Chicago Symphony		I
__ MMO CD 3514		Mason Jones, Philadelphia Orch.		I
__ MMO CD 3515		Myron Bloom, Cleveland Symphony		A
__ MMO CD 3516		Dale Clevenger, Chicago Symphony		A
__ MMO CD 3517		Mason Jones, Philadelphia Orch.		I
__ MMO CD 3518		Myron Bloom, Cleveland Symphony		A
__ MMO CD 3519		Dale Clevenger, Chicago Symphony		I

The repertoire and editions used in the Laureate Series correspond to the approved music lists of various Music Education Associations and may be performed as contest solos in State Music Festivals. Contest regulations, such as time limitations have been taken into consideration.

MUSIC MINUS ONE COMPACT DISC CATALOG

Music Minus One ALTO SAX Compact Discs

___ MMO CD 4101 Easy Solos, Student Editions, Beginning Level vol. 1
___ MMO CD 4102 Easy Solos, Student Editions, Beginning Level vol. 2
___ MMO CD 4103 Easy Jazz Duets, Student Editions, 1-3 years
___ MMO CD 4104 For Saxes Only, Arr. by Bob Wilber

Choice selections for the Alto Sax, drawn from the very best solo literature for the instrument. The pieces are performed by the foremost virtuosi of our time, artists affiliated with the New York Philharmonic, Boston, Chicago, Cleveland and Philadelphia Orchestras, The Juilliard School, Curtis Institute of Music, Indiana University, University of Toronto and Metropolitan Opera Orchestra.

___ Beginning	Intermediate Advanced	Level
___ MMO CD 4111	Paul Brodie, Canadian Soloist	B
___ MMO CD 4112	Vincent Abato, Metropolitan Opera Orch.	B
___ MMO CD 4113	Paul Brodie, Canadian Soloist	I
___ MMO CD 4114	Vincent Abato, Metropolitan Opera Orch.	I
___ MMO CD 4115	Paul Brodie, Canadian Soloist, Clinician	A
___ MMO CD 4116	Vincent Abato, Metropolitan Opera Orch.	A
___ MMO CD 4117	Paul Brodie, Canadian Soloist, Clinician	A
___ MMO CD 4118	Vincent Abato, Metropolitan Opera Orch.	A

The repertoire and editions used in the Laureate Series correspond to the approved music lists of various Music Education Associations and may be performed as contest solos in State Music Festivals. Contest regulations, such as time limitations have been taken into consideration.

Music Minus One TENOR SAX Compact Discs

___ MMO CD 4201 Easy Tenor Sax Solos, Student Editions, 1-3 years
___ MMO CD 4202 Easy Tenor Sax Solos, Student Editions, 1-3 years
___ MMO CD 4203 Easy Jazz Duets with Rhythm Section, Beginning Level
___ MMO CD 4204 For Saxes Only, Arr. by Bob Wilber

Music Minus One TROMBONE Compact Discs

___ MMO CD 3901 Easy Solos, Student Editions, Beginning Level vol. 1
___ MMO CD 3902 Easy Solos, Student Editions, Beginning Level vol. 2
___ MMO CD 3903 Easy Jazz Duets, Student Editions, 1-3 years

Choice selections for the Trombone, drawn from the very best solo literature for the instrument. The pieces are performed by the foremost virtuosi of our time, artists affiliated with the New York Philharmonic, Boston, Chicago, Cleveland and Philadelphia Orchestras, The Juilliard School, Curtis Institute of Music, Indiana University, University of Toronto and Metropolitan Opera Orchestra.

Beginning	Intermediate Advanced	Level
___ MMO CD 3904	Baroque Brass & Beyond	
___ MMO CD 3905	Music For Brass Ensemble	
___ MMO CD 3911	Per Brevig, Metropolitan Opera Orch.	B
___ MMO CD 3912	Jay Friedman, Chicago Symphony	B
___ MMO CD 3913	Keith Brown, Soloist, Prof. Indiana Univ.	I
___ MMO CD 3914	Jay Friedman, Chicago Symphony	I
___ MMO CD 3915	Keith Brown, Soloist, Prof. Indiana Univ.	A
___ MMO CD 3916	Per Brevig, Metropolitan Opera Orch.	A
___ MMO CD 3917	Keith Brown, Soloist, Prof. Indiana Univ.	A
___ MMO CD 3918	Jay Friedman, Chicago Symphony	A
___ MMO CD 3919	Per Brevig, Metropolitan Opera Orch.	A

The repertoire and editions used in the Laureate Series correspond to the approved music lists of various Music Education Associations and may be performed as contest solos in State Music Festivals. Contest regulations, such as time limitations have been taken into consideration.

Music Minus One BROADWAY Shows

___ MMO CD 1016	LES MISERABLES/PHANTOM OF THE OPERA	
___ MMO CD 1067	GUYS AND DOLLS	
___ MMO CD 1100	WEST SIDE STORY	2 CD Set
___ MMO CD 1130	ANDREW LLOYD WEBBER HITS	
___ MMO CD 1151	JEKYLL & HYDE	
___ MMO CD 1173	CAMELOT	
___ MMO CD 1174	MY FAIR LADY	2 CD Set
___ MMO CD 1175	OKLAHOMA	
___ MMO CD 1176	THE SOUND OF MUSIC	2 CD Set
___ MMO CD 1177	SOUTH PACIFIC	
___ MMO CD 1178	THE KING AND I	2 CD Set
___ MMO CD 1179	THE FIDDLER ON THE ROOF	
___ MMO CD 1180	CAROUSEL	
___ MMO CD 1181	PORGY AND BESS	
___ MMO CD 1183	THE MUSIC MAN	
___ MMO CD 1184	SHOWBOAT	
___ MMO CD 1187	HELLO DOLLY	2 CD Set
___ MMO CD 1186	ANNIE GET YOUR GUN	2 CD Set
___ MMO CD 1189	OLIVER	2 CD Set
___ MMO CD 1193	SUNSET BOULEVARD	
___ MMO CD 1197	SMOKEY JOE'S CAFE	
___ MMO CD 1198	WALT DISNEY FAVORITE SONGS	

Music Minus One OBOE Compact Discs

___ MMO CD 3400 Albinoni Three Oboe Concerti Opus 7 No. 3, No. 6, Opus 9 No. 2
___ MMO CD 3401 3 Oboe Concerti: Handel, Telemann, Vivaldi
___ MMO CD 3402 Mozart/Stamitz Oboe Quartets in F major (K.370; Op.8 #3)

Music Minus One DRUMMER Compact Discs

___ MMO CD 5001 MODERN JAZZ DRUMMING, 2 CD Set
___ MMO CD 5002 FOR DRUMMERS ONLY!
___ MMO CD 5003 WIPE-OUT!
___ MMO CD 5004 SIT IN!
*MMO CD 5005 DRUM STAR
*MMO CD 5006 DRUMPADSTICKSKIN
*MMO CD 5007 LIGHT MY FIRE
*MMO CD 5008 FIRE AND RAIN
*MMO CD 5009 CLASSICAL PERCUSSION, 2 CD Set
*Winter '95/Spring '96 Release

Music Minus One BANJO Compact Discs

___ MMO CD 4401 Bluegrass Banjo

Music Minus One BASS VIOLIN Compact Discs

___ MMO CD 4301 Beginning & Intermediate Bass Solos
___ MMO CD 4302 Intermediate & Advanced Bass Solos

Music Minus One INSTRUCTION METHODS

___ MMO CD 7001 Rutgers University Music Dictation Series
                6 CD Set   Deluxe Album $98.00
___ MMO CD 7002 The Music Teacher
___ MMO CD 7003 The Complete Guitar Method
___ MMO CD 7004 Evolution Of The Blues
___ MMO CD 7005 Art Of Improvisation, vol. 1
___ MMO CD 7006 Art Of Improvisation, vol. 2

Music Minus One VIOLIN Compact Discs

___ MMO CD 3100 Bruch Violin Concerto in Gm
___ MMO CD 3101 Mendelssohn Violin Concerto in Em
___ MMO CD 3102 Tschaikovsky Violin Concerto in D, Opus 35
___ MMO CD 3103 J.S. Bach "Double" Concerto in Dm
___ MMO CD 3104 J.S. Bach Violin Concerti in Am/E
___ MMO CD 3105 J.S. Bach Brandenburg Concerti Nos. 4 and 5
___ MMO CD 3106 J.S. Bach Brandenburg No. 2/Triple Concerto
___ MMO CD 3107 J.S. Bach Concerto in Dm
___ MMO CD 3108 Brahms Violin Concerto in D, Opus 77
___ MMO CD 3109 Chausson Poeme/Schubert Rondo
___ MMO CD 3110 Lalo Symphonie Espagnole
___ MMO CD 3111 Mozart Concerto in D/Vivaldi Concerto in Am
___ MMO CD 3112 Mozart Violin Concerto in A, K.219
___ MMO CD 3113 Wieniawski Concerto in D/Sarasate Zigeunerweisen
___ MMO CD 3114 Viotti Concerto No. 22
___ MMO CD 3115 Beethoven Two Romances/"Spring" Sonata
___ MMO CD 3116 St. Saëns Intro & Rondo Cap./Mozart Serenade & Adagio
___ MMO CD 3117 Beethoven Violin Concerto in D major, Opus 61
___ MMO CD 3118 The Concertmaster Solos from Symphonic Works
___ MMO CD 3119 Air On A G String Favorite Encores for Orchestra
___ MMO CD 3120 Concert Pieces For The Serious Violinist
___ MMO CD 3121 Eighteenth Century Violin Music
___ MMO CD 3122 Violin Favorites With Orchestra Vol. 1 (Easy)
___ MMO CD 3123 Violin Favorites With Orchestra Vol. 2 (Moderate)
___ MMO CD 3124 Violin Favorites With Orchestra Vol. 3 (Mod. Diff.)
___ MMO CD 3125 The Three B's: Bach/Beethoven/Brahms
___ MMO CD 3126 Vivaldi Concerti in Am, D, Am Opus 3 No. 6,9,8
___ MMO CD 3127 Vivaldi "The Four Seasons" 2 CD set $29.98 each
___ MMO CD 3128 Vivaldi "La Tempesta di Mare" Opus 8 No. 5
                Albinoni: Violin Concerto in A
___ MMO CD 3129 Vivaldi: Violin Concerto Opus 3 No. 12
                Vivaldi Violin Concerto Opus 8, No. 6 "Il Piacere"
___ MMO CD 3130 Schubert Three Sonatina, Opus 137
___ MMO CD 3131 Haydn String Quartet No. 1 in G, Op. 76
___ MMO CD 3132 Haydn String Quartet No. 2 in d, Op. 76
___ MMO CD 3133 Haydn String Quartet No. 3 in C, Op. 76 "Emperor"
___ MMO CD 3134 Haydn String Quartet No. 4 in Bb, Op. 76 "Sunrise"
___ MMO CD 3135 Haydn String Quartet No. 5 in D, Op. 76
___ MMO CD 3136 Haydn String Quartet No. 6 in Eb, Op. 76

MUSIC MINUS ONE COMPACT DISC CATALOG

Music Minus One CLARINET Compact Discs

__ MMO CD 3201 Mozart Clarinet Concerto in A major
__ MMO CD 3202 Weber Clarinet Concerto No. 1 in F minor, Op. 73
        Stamitz Clarinet Concerto No. 3 in Bb major
__ MMO CD 3203 Spohr Clarinet Concerto No. 1 in C minor, Op. 26
__ MMO CD 3204 Weber Clarinet Concertino, Opus 26
__ MMO CD 3205 First Chair Clarinet Solos *Orchestral Excerpts*
__ MMO CD 3206 The Art Of The Solo Clarinet *Orchestral Excerpts*
__ MMO CD 3207 Mozart: Quintet for Clarinet and Strings in A, K.581
__ MMO CD 3208 Brahms: Sonatas Opus 120, Nos. 1 & 2
__ MMO CD 3209 Weber: Grand Duo Concertant - Wagner: Adagio
__ MMO CD 3210 Schumann Fantasy Pieces, Opus 73, Three Romances
__ MMO CD 3211 Easy Clarinet Solos, Student Editions 1-3 years
__ MMO CD 3212 Easy Clarinet Solos, Student Editions 1-3 years, vol. 2
__ MMO CD 3213 Easy Jazz Duets, Student Editions, 1-3 years

Choice selections for the Clarinet, drawn from the very best solo literature for the instrument. The pieces are performed by the foremost virtuosi of our time, artists affiliated with the New York Philharmonic, Boston, Chicago, Cleveland and Philadelphia Orchestras, The Juilliard School, Curtis Institute of Music, Indiana University, University of Toronto and Metropolitan Opera Orchestra.

Beginning	Intermediate Advanced	Level
__ MMO CD 3221	Jerome Bunke, Clinician	B
__ MMO CD 3222	Harold Wright, Boston Symphony	B
__ MMO CD 3223	Stanley Drucker, N.Y. Philharmonic	I
__ MMO CD 3224	Jerome Bunke, Clinician	I
__ MMO CD 3225	Stanley Drucker, N.Y. Philharmonic	A
__ MMO CD 3226	Harold Wright, Boston Symphony	A
__ MMO CD 3227	Stanley Drucker, N.Y. Philharmonic	I
__ MMO CD 3228	Stanley Drucker, N.Y. Philharmonic	A
__ MMO CD 3229	Harold Wright, Boston Symphony	A

The repertoire and editions used in the Laureate Series correspond to the approved music lists of various Music Education Associations and may be performed as contest solos in State Music Festivals. Contest regulations, such as time limitations have been taken into consideration.

Music Minus One TRUMPET Compact Discs

__ MMO CD 3801 3 Trumpet Concerti   Handel/Telemann/Vivaldi
__ MMO CD 3802 Easy Solos, Student Edition, Beginning Level vol. 1
__ MMO CD 3803 Easy Solos, Student Edition, Beginning Level vol. 2
__ MMO CD 3804 Easy Jazz Duets with Rhythm Section, Beginning Level
__ MMO CD 3805 Music for Brass Ensemble
__ MMO CD 3806 First Chair Trumpet Solos
__ MMO CD 3807 The Art Of The Solo Trumpet
__ MMO CD 3808 Baroque Brass And Beyond
__ MMO CD 3809 The Arban Duets

Choice selections for the Trumpet, drawn from the very best solo literature for the instrument. The pieces are performed by the foremost virtuosi of our time, artists affiliated with the New York Philharmonic, Boston, Chicago, Cleveland and Philadelphia Orchestras, The Juilliard School, Curtis Institute of Music, Indiana University, University of Toronto and Metropolitan Opera Orchestra.

Beginning	Intermediate Advanced	Level
__ MMO CD 3811	Gerard Schwarz, N.Y. Philharmonic	B
__ MMO CD 3812	Armando Ghitalla, Boston Symphony	B
__ MMO CD 3813	Robert Nagel, Soloist, NY Brass Ensemble	I
__ MMO CD 3814	Gerard Schwarz, N.Y. Philharmonic	I
__ MMO CD 3815	Robert Nagel, Soloist NY Brass Ensemble	A
__ MMO CD 3816	Armando Ghitalla, Boston Symphony	I
__ MMO CD 3817	Gerard Schwarz, N.Y. Philharmonic	I
__ MMO CD 3818	Robert Nagel, Soloist, NY Brass Ensemble	A
__ MMO CD 3819	Armando Ghitalla, Boston Symphony	A
__ MMO CD 3820	Raymond Crisara, Concert Soloist	B
__ MMO CD 3821	Raymond Crisara, Concert Soloist	B
__ MMO CD 3822	Raymond Crisara, Concert Soloist	I

The repertoire and editions used in the Laureate Series correspond to the approved music lists of various Music Education Associations and may be performed as contest solos in State Music Festivals. Contest regulations, such as time limitations have been taken into consideration.

MUSIC MINUS ONE 50 Executive Boulevard • Elmsford New York 10523-1325